MUFFIN SAMPLER

A Collection of Favorite Muffin Recipes

by Jan Siegrist

THE NEW ENGLAND PRESS, INC.

©1989 by Jan Siegrist
ALL RIGHTS RESERVED

For additional copies write to:
   The New England Press, Inc.
   P.O. Box 575
   Shelburne, Vermont 05482

Other Samplers also available:
   Apple, Blueberry, Casserole,
   Cheese and Dairy, Cookie, Maple,
   New England, Seafood, Strawberry,
   Whole Grain, Zucchini

Written and illustrated by
Jan Seygal Siegrist

ISBN 0-933050-67-4

PRINTED IN THE UNITED STATES OF AMERICA

CONTENTS

Introduction, 5

Fruit Muffins

- Almond Apricot Muffins, 9
- Apple Streusel Muffins, 10
- Sugar-Top Applesauce Muffins, 11
- Spicy Banana Nut Muffins, 13
- Old-Fashioned Blueberry Muffins, 14
- Black Cherry Pecan Muffins, 15
- Cranberry Nut Muffins, 16
- Cranberry Sauce Muffins, 17
- Fresh Peach Muffins, 18
- Pineapple Muffins, 20

Vegetable Muffins

- Swirled Carrot Muffins, 21
- Whole Wheat Carrot Muffins, 23
- Confetti Corn Muffins, 24
- Mexican Muffins, 25
- Pumpkin Pecan Muffins, 26
- Lemon Zucchini Muffins, 28

✿ Whole Grain Muffins
- Breakfast Bran Muffins, 29
- Refrigerator Raisin Bran Muffins, 30
- Easy Oat Bran Muffins, 31
- Oatmeal Raisin Muffins, 32
- Healthy Whole Grain Muffins, 34
- Honey Whole Wheat Dinner Muffins, 35
- Shredded Wheat Muffins, 36

✿ Dessert Muffins
- Aloha Muffins, 37
- Deluxe Chocolate Chip Muffins, 38
- Coffeecake Muffins, 39
- Fruit Cocktail Muffins, 41
- Stuffed Gingerbread Muffins, 42
- Glazed Lemon Nut Muffins, 44
- Mincemeat Muffins, 45
- Peanut Butter Muffins, 46

✿ And Furthermore
- Basic Muffin and Variations, 47
- Savory Cheddar Muffins, 48

INTRODUCTION

> MUFFINS. What better way to start the morning than with a fresh-baked muffin warm from the oven? Loaded with nourishing and delicious ingredients, muffins are not just for breakfast or special occasions — they make a healthy addition to any meal. Quick and easy to fix, they freeze well and make good travelers. The muffin is the ideal convenience food to pack for school lunches, office coffee breaks, and snacks — especially on long automobile trips and when you are backpacking or biking.

> Muffins can be baked in a variety of sizes, ranging from dainty, gem-size muffins, about 1 inch in diameter, to jumbo muffins, about 3 inches in diameter. The recipes in this book call for the standard, full-size muffin pan with 2 to 2½-inch diameter cups. Custard cups or metal canning rings lined with paper baking cups and placed on a cookie sheet can also be used. Baking

times for larger or smaller pans vary accordingly.

- For successful muffin baking, there are a few important guidelines to remember. First and foremost, beware of overmixing the batter. Mix the dry and wet ingredients separately; combine them quickly, stirring with a gentle touch until just moist. The batter should still be a little lumpy and break into globs. Overmixing will toughen the dough, causing cracks and tunnels and a coarse texture. On the other hand, undermixing will result in a muffin with a flat top, low volume, and crumbly texture. Good muffins should have round tops, straight sides, a moist, even-textured crumb, and no tunnels.

- Have the muffin pans lightly greased or lined with paper muffin cups before combining the wet and dry ingredients. Once the batter is mixed, fill the cups immediately. For normal-size muffins, fill the cups about 2/3 full with the batter. For muffins with crusty, over-sized tops, fill the cups almost to the top. (Be sure to grease the top of the tins to prevent sticking.) Fill any empty cups with water to prevent the pans from scorching and to ensure even baking.

▶ The correct oven temperature is extremely important when baking muffins. Too cool an oven will result in a muffin with a flat top; whereas if the oven temperature is too hot, the muffin will form a cracked, wobbly, asymmetrical peak. Most muffin recipes call for a preheated, hot oven, about 400°F, and a baking time of 20-25 minutes. To test for doneness, insert a sharp knife or wooden pick near the center of the muffin. If it comes out clean, the muffin is done. Cool the muffins on a wire rack for about 5 minutes before removing them from the pan.

❁ Muffins are best served warm, fresh from the oven; however, they can be frozen and reheated when needed. Allow the muffins to cool completely, then wrap them tightly in foil or plastic wrap, place in plastic bags, and freeze for up to 3 months. To reheat, loosely wrap the muffins in foil and place them in a preheated 425°F oven for about 10 minutes or in an electric skillet with a tight lid over low heat for 10-20 minutes. Frozen muffins can also be reheated in a microwave oven following the manufacturer's instructions for the oven being used.

❁ The versatile muffin can be a lifesaver when unexpected guests drop by or when the kids come running in for an after-school snack. So whether you prefer to bake a batch of Fresh Peach Muffins or a dozen Deluxe Chocolate Chip, you're sure to find a recipe in this book to get you started.

Almond Apricot Muffins

1 can (12 ounces) apricot nectar (1½ cups)
½ cup chopped dried apricots
¼ cup butter or margarine
2 cups all-purpose flour
½ cup sugar
1 tablespoon baking powder
1 egg
1 teaspoon almond extract
½ cup chopped almonds

In a medium-size saucepan, combine the nectar and apricots; heat to boiling. Remove from the heat; stir in the butter; cool. In a large bowl, combine the flour, sugar, and baking powder. In a separate bowl, beat together the egg and almond extract; stir in the apricot mixture. Add to the flour mixture; stir until just moist. Fill greased muffin cups ⅔ full with the batter. Sprinkle the almonds over the batter in each cup. Bake in a preheated 400°F oven for 20-25 minutes. Cool on a wire rack for 5 minutes; remove from the pan. Makes 12 muffins.

Apple Streusel Muffins

2 cups all-purpose flour
1/4 cup sugar
1 tablespoon baking powder
1 egg
1 cup milk
1/4 cup vegetable oil
1 medium-size apple, peeled and chopped
* Streusel

In a large bowl, combine the flour, sugar, and baking powder. In a separate bowl, beat together the egg, milk, and oil; add to the flour mixture. Stir until just moist; fold in the apple. Fill greased muffin cups about 1/3 full with the batter. Add 2 teaspoons of Streusel to each cup; top with the remaining batter to fill each cup 2/3 full. Sprinkle the remaining Streusel over the batter in each cup. Bake in a preheated 400°F oven for 20-25 minutes. Cool on a wire rack for 5 minutes; remove from the pan. Makes 12 muffins.

* Streusel: In a small bowl, mix 1/2 cup

all-purpose flour, ⅓ cup brown sugar, 1 teaspoon cinnamon, ¼ cup chopped nuts, and ¼ cup melted butter until crumbly.

Sugar-Top Applesauce Muffins

¾ cup raisins
½ cup water
1 cup all-purpose flour
1 cup whole wheat flour
2 teaspoons baking powder
½ teaspoon baking soda
½ teaspoon nutmeg
1 egg
½ cup sugar
¼ cup vegetable oil
1 cup unsweetened applesauce
2 tablespoons sugar
½ teaspoon cinnamon

➊ Soak the raisins in the water for at least 15 minutes. In a large bowl, combine the all-purpose flour, whole wheat flour, baking powder, baking soda, and nutmeg.

In a separate bowl, beat together the egg and ½ cup sugar until fluffy; stir in the oil and applesauce. Add to the flour mixture; stir until just moist. Fold in the raisins with their liquid. Fill greased muffin cups about ⅔ full with the batter. Combine the remaining 2 tablespoons sugar and cinnamon; sprinkle over the batter in each cup. Bake in a preheated 375°F oven for 20-25 minutes. Cool on a wire rack for 5 minutes; remove from the pan. Makes 12 muffins.

Spicy Banana Nut Muffins

1 3/4 cups all-purpose flour
1/3 cup brown sugar
1 tablespoon baking powder
1 teaspoon cinnamon
1/4 teaspoon nutmeg
1/4 teaspoon cloves
2 eggs, beaten
1/3 cup butter or margarine, melted
1/2 cup milk
1 cup mashed, ripe bananas (about 2 bananas)
1/2 cup chopped nuts

In a large bowl, combine the flour, sugar, baking powder, cinnamon, nutmeg, and cloves. In a separate bowl, mix together the eggs, butter, milk, and bananas; add to the flour mixture. Stir until just moist. Fold in the nuts. Fill greased muffin cups about 2/3 full with the batter. Bake in a preheated 400°F oven for 20-25 minutes. Cool on a wire rack for 5 minutes; remove from the pan. Makes 12 muffins.

Delicious for breakfast with a glass of juice.

Old-Fashioned Blueberry Muffins

¼ cup butter or margarine
¼ cup sugar
2 eggs
2 cups all-purpose flour
4 teaspoons baking powder
1 cup milk
1½ cups blueberries
1 tablespoon all-purpose flour

In a large bowl, cream together the butter and sugar. Add the eggs; beat well. In a separate bowl, combine 2 cups flour and the baking powder. Add to the creamed mixture alternately with the milk. Stir until just moist. Toss the berries with the remaining 1 tablespoon flour; fold into the batter. Fill greased muffin cups about ⅔ full with the batter. Bake in a preheated 375°F oven for 20-25 minutes. Cool on a wire rack for 5 minutes; remove from the pan. Makes 12 muffins.

Best served warm with whipped butter.

Black Cherry Pecan Muffins

2 cups all-purpose flour
1 tablespoon baking powder
½ teaspoon nutmeg
1 cup chopped and pitted dark cherries
   (or canned cherries, well-drained and
   patted dry)
⅓ cup butter or margarine
½ cup sugar
2 eggs, beaten
¾ cup milk
12 pecan halves

In a large bowl, combine the flour, baking powder, and nutmeg. Add the cherries; toss to coat. In a separate bowl, cream together the butter and sugar; stir in the eggs and milk. Add to the flour mixture; stir until just moist. Fill greased muffin cups about ⅔ full with the batter. Top each with a pecan half. Bake in a preheated 400°F oven for 20-25 minutes. Cool on a wire rack for 5 minutes; remove from the pan. Makes 12 muffins.

Cranberry Nut Muffins

2½ cups all-purpose flour
¾ cup sugar
4 teaspoons baking powder
1 cup milk
2 eggs
¼ cup shortening, melted
1 cup coarsely chopped cranberries
½ cup chopped walnuts
1 tablespoon grated orange peel

In a large bowl, combine the flour, sugar, and baking powder. In a separate bowl, beat together the milk, eggs, and shortening; add to the flour mixture. Stir until just moist. Fold in the chopped cranberries, walnuts, and orange peel. Fill greased muffin cups about ⅔ full with the batter. Bake in a preheated 400°F oven for 20-25 minutes. Cool on a wire rack for 5 minutes; remove from the pan. Makes 12 muffins.

Serve warm with whipped cream cheese.

Cranberry Sauce Muffins

2 cups all-purpose flour
1/3 cup sugar
1 1/2 teaspoons baking powder
1/2 teaspoon baking soda
1 egg
1/4 cup vegetable oil
3/4 cup orange juice
1 tablespoon grated orange peel
1/2 cup chopped pecans
1/2 cup whole cranberry sauce

In a large bowl, combine the flour, sugar, baking powder, and baking soda. In a separate bowl, beat together the egg, oil, juice, and orange peel; add to the flour mixture. Stir until just moist. Fold in the pecans. Fill greased muffin cups about 1/3 full with the batter. Add 2 teaspoons cranberry sauce to each cup; top with the remaining batter to fill each cup 2/3 full. Bake in a preheated 400°F oven for 15-20 minutes. Cool on a wire rack for 5 minutes; remove from the pan. Makes 12 muffins.

Fresh Peach Muffins

½ cup milk
½ cup sour cream
1 cup rolled oats
⅓ cup butter or margarine
½ cup brown sugar
1 egg
1½ cups all-purpose flour
1 teaspoon baking powder
½ teaspoon baking soda
½ teaspoon cinnamon
¼ teaspoon cloves
¼ teaspoon nutmeg
1½ cups peeled and coarsely chopped fresh peaches

In a large bowl, combine the milk, sour cream, and oats; let stand for 15 minutes. In a separate bowl, cream together the butter and brown sugar; beat in the egg. Add to the oatmeal mixture; mix well. Combine the flour, baking powder, baking soda, cinnamon, cloves, and nutmeg. Add to the oatmeal mixture; stir until just moist. Fold in the chopped peaches. Fill greased muffin cups about $\frac{2}{3}$ full with the batter. Bake in a preheated 400°F oven for 20-25 minutes. Cool on a wire rack for 5 minutes; remove from the pan. Makes 12 muffins.

To substitute canned peaches, drain 1 can (16 ounces) cling peaches, reserving $\frac{1}{2}$ cup peach syrup. Replace the milk with the syrup and decrease the brown sugar to $\frac{1}{4}$ cup. Coarsely chop the drained peaches before folding into the batter.

Celebrate summer when fresh peaches are in season with these moist muffins.

Pineapple Muffins

2¼ cups all-purpose flour
2 teaspoons baking powder
½ teaspoon baking soda
⅓ cup butter or margarine
½ cup sugar
1 egg
1 teaspoon vanilla extract
1 can (8¼ ounces) unsweetened crushed pineapple
¼ cup chopped nuts
¼ cup chopped maraschino cherries, well-drained (optional)

🍄 In a large bowl, combine the flour, baking powder, and baking soda. In a separate bowl, cream together the butter and sugar; beat in the egg and vanilla. Drain the pineapple, reserving the liquid. Add enough water to the liquid to make 1 cup; stir into the egg mixture. Add to the flour mixture; stir until just moist. Fold in the drained pineapple, nuts, and cherries. Fill greased muffin cups about ⅔ full with the batter. Bake in a preheated 400°F oven for 20-25 minutes. Cool on a wire rack for 5 minutes; remove from the pan. Makes 12 muffins.

Swirled Carrot Muffins

2 cups all-purpose flour
½ cup brown sugar
1 tablespoon baking powder
1 teaspoon cinnamon
¼ teaspoon nutmeg
1 cup finely shredded carrots
½ cup shredded unsweetened coconut
2 eggs
⅓ cup vegetable oil
¾ cup milk
1 package (3 ounces) cream cheese, softened
3 tablespoons milk
1 teaspoon vanilla extract

In a large bowl, combine the flour, sugar, baking powder, cinnamon, nutmeg, carrots, and coconut. In a separate bowl, beat together the eggs, oil, and ¾ cup milk; add to the flour mixture. Stir until just moist. Fill greased muffin cups ⅓ full with the batter. In a small bowl, blend together the cream cheese, the remaining 3 tablespoons milk, and vanilla. Add about 1 tablespoon of the mixture to each muffin cup; add the remaining batter to fill each cup about ⅔ full. Using a knife, cut through the batter in each cup to swirl the filling. Bake in a preheated 400°F oven for 20-25 minutes. Cool on a wire rack for 5 minutes; remove from the pan. Makes 12 muffins.

No need to butter these cheese-swirled fancy muffins.

Whole Wheat Carrot Muffins

1 cup whole wheat flour
1 cup all-purpose flour
2 teaspoons baking powder
½ teaspoon baking soda
2 eggs, beaten
½ cup milk
¼ cup vegetable oil
½ cup molasses
1 cup finely shredded carrots
½ cup chopped dates

In a large bowl, combine the whole wheat flour, all-purpose flour, baking powder, and baking soda. In a separate bowl, mix together the eggs, milk, oil, and molasses; add to the flour mixture. Stir until just moist. Stir in the carrots and dates. Fill greased muffin cups ⅔ full with the batter. Bake in a preheated 400°F oven for 20-25 minutes. Cool on a wire rack for 5 minutes; remove from the pan. Makes 12 muffins.

Pack these moist muffins for lunch.

Confetti Corn Muffins

1 cup yellow cornmeal
1 cup all-purpose flour
1 teaspoon dried basil
2 tablespoons sugar
1 tablespoon baking powder
2 eggs
1 cup milk
¼ cup butter or margarine, melted
½ cup finely chopped green pepper
½ cup shredded carrot
½ cup finely chopped onion

In a large bowl, combine the cornmeal, flour, basil, sugar, and baking powder. In a separate bowl, beat together the eggs, milk, and butter; add to the flour mixture. Stir until just moist. Fold in the pepper, carrot, and onion. Fill greased muffin cups about ⅔ full with the batter. Bake in a preheated 400°F oven for 20-25 minutes. Cool on a wire rack for 5 minutes; remove from the pan. Makes 12 muffins.

Mexican Muffins

1¼ cups all-purpose flour
¾ cup yellow cornmeal
1 tablespoon baking powder
½ cup fresh or drained, whole-kernel canned corn
2 eggs, slightly beaten
½ cup milk
½ cup salsa
3 tablespoons butter or margarine, melted
½ cup shredded Monterey jack cheese

In a large bowl, combine the flour, cornmeal, baking powder, and corn. In a separate bowl, mix together the eggs, milk, salsa, and butter. Add to the flour mixture; stir until just moist. Fill greased muffin cups about ⅔ full with the batter. Sprinkle the cheese over the batter in each cup. Bake in a preheated 400°F oven for 20-25 minutes. Cool on a wire rack for 5 minutes; remove from the pan. Makes 12 muffins.

Serve with soup and salad for Sunday supper.

Pumpkin Pecan Muffins

2 cups all-purpose flour
1 teaspoon baking powder
$\frac{1}{2}$ teaspoon baking soda
1 teaspoon cinnamon
$\frac{1}{2}$ teaspoon allspice
$\frac{1}{3}$ cup chopped pecans
2 eggs, beaten
1 teaspoon vanilla extract
1 cup canned cooked pumpkin
$\frac{1}{3}$ cup vegetable oil
$\frac{1}{4}$ cup milk
$\frac{1}{2}$ cup brown sugar
* Topping

In a large bowl, combine the flour, baking powder, baking soda, cinnamon, allspice, and nuts. In a separate bowl, mix together the eggs, vanilla, pumpkin, oil, milk, and brown sugar; add to the flour mixture. Stir until just moist. Fill greased muffin cups about $\frac{2}{3}$ full with the batter. Sprinkle the Topping over the batter in each cup.

Bake in a preheated 400°F oven for 20-25 minutes. Cool on a wire rack for 5 minutes; remove from the pan. Makes 12 muffins.

*<u>Topping</u>: In a small bowl, mix together 2 tablespoons rolled oats, 2 tablespoons all-purpose flour, 2 tablespoons brown sugar, 3 tablespoons chopped pecans, and 1 teaspoon cinnamon. Cut in 3 tablespoons butter or margarine until crumbly.

A nutty oatmeal topping makes these spicy pumpkin muffins special.

Lemon Zucchini Muffins

2 cups all-purpose flour
½ cup sugar
1 tablespoon baking powder
1 tablespoon grated lemon peel
½ teaspoon nutmeg
½ cup chopped walnuts
½ cup golden raisins
2 eggs, beaten
½ cup milk
½ cup vegetable oil
1 cup shredded zucchini

In a large bowl, combine the flour, sugar, baking powder, lemon peel, and nutmeg; stir in the nuts and raisins. In a separate bowl, mix together the eggs, milk, and oil. Stir in the zucchini. Add to the flour mixture; stir until just moist. Fill greased muffin cups about ⅔ full with the batter. Bake in a preheated 375°F oven for 20-25 minutes. Cool on a wire rack for 5 minutes; remove from the pan. Makes 12 muffins.

Breakfast Bran Muffins

1 cup shredded bran cereal (e.g. All-Bran®, 100% Bran®, etc.)
1 cup orange juice
1 egg
¼ cup vegetable oil
1 cup all-purpose flour
2 teaspoons baking powder
½ teaspoon baking soda
¼ cup brown sugar
½ cup raisins or chopped dates

In a large bowl, combine the cereal and juice; let stand until the cereal is softened, about 5 minutes. Beat in the egg and oil. In a separate bowl, combine the flour, baking powder, baking soda, brown sugar, and raisins or dates. Add to the cereal mixture; stir until just moist. Fill greased muffin cups about ⅔ full with the batter. Bake in a preheated 400°F oven for 20-25 minutes. Cool on a wire rack for 5 minutes; remove from the pan. Makes 12 muffins.

Refrigerator Raisin Bran Muffins

1 package (15 ounces) Raisin Bran® cereal
5 cups all-purpose flour
2½ cups sugar
5 teaspoons baking soda
4 eggs, beaten
1 quart buttermilk
1 cup vegetable oil

In a large bowl, combine the cereal, flour, sugar, and baking soda. In a separate bowl, combine the eggs, buttermilk, and oil; mix well. Add to the bran mixture; stir until just moist. Use immediately or store in a tightly covered container in the refrigerator for up to 6 weeks. To bake, fill greased muffin cups about ⅔ full with the batter. Bake in a preheated 400°F oven for 15-20 minutes. Cool on a wire rack for 5 minutes; remove from the pan. Makes about 48 muffins.

Keep a batch of this batter in your refrigerator for freshly baked muffins every day.

Easy Oat Bran Muffins

¾ cup oat bran
½ cup whole wheat flour
½ cup all-purpose flour
¼ cup brown sugar
2 teaspoons baking powder
½ teaspoon cinnamon
1 egg
¾ cup milk
2 tablespoons vegetable oil
1 small apple, finely chopped
½ cup raisins

In a large bowl, combine the oat bran, whole wheat flour, all-purpose flour, sugar, baking powder, and cinnamon. In a separate bowl, beat together the egg, milk, and oil; add to the flour mixture. Stir until just moist. Fold in the apple and raisins. Fill greased muffin cups about ⅔ full with the batter. Bake in a preheated 400° F oven for 15-20 minutes. Cool on a wire rack for 5 minutes; remove from the pan. Makes 12 muffins.

Oatmeal Raisin Muffins

1 cup buttermilk or sour milk*
1 cup rolled oats
½ cup raisins
½ teaspoon cinnamon
1 egg
⅓ cup butter or margarine, melted
¼ cup brown sugar
1 cup all-purpose flour
1 teaspoon baking powder
½ teaspoon baking soda

🍄 Combine the buttermilk, oats, raisins, and cinnamon; let stand until the liquid is absorbed, about ½ hour. In a large bowl, beat together the egg, butter, and brown sugar; stir in the oat mixture. In a separate bowl, combine the flour, baking powder, and baking soda; add to the oat mixture. Stir until just moist. Fill greased muffin cups about ⅔ full with the batter. Bake in a preheated 400°F oven for 20-25 minutes. Cool on a wire rack for

5 minutes; remove from the pan. Makes 12 muffins.

* To make sour milk, place 1 tablespoon lemon juice or vinegar in a measuring cup. Add enough milk to make 1 cup; mix well. Let stand for 10 minutes.

Oats give these muffins a lovely texture.

Healthy Whole Grain Muffins

½ cup whole wheat flour
½ cup all-purpose flour
¼ cup shredded bran cereal (e.g. All-Bran®, 100% Bran, etc.)
¼ cup wheat germ
¼ cup rolled oats
1 teaspoon baking soda
½ teaspoon cinnamon
½ cup raisins or chopped prunes
1 egg, beaten
¼ cup vegetable oil
⅓ cup pure maple syrup
1 cup plain yogurt

In a large bowl, combine the whole wheat flour, all-purpose flour, bran cereal, wheat germ, oats, baking soda, cinnamon, and raisins. In a separate bowl, mix together the egg, oil, maple syrup, and yogurt; add to the flour mixture. Stir until just moist. Fill greased muffin cups about ⅔ full with the batter. Bake in a preheated 400°F oven for 20-25 minutes. Cool on a wire rack for 5 minutes; remove from the pan. Makes 12 muffins.

Honey Whole Wheat Dinner Muffins

1 cup whole wheat flour
1 cup all-purpose flour
1 tablespoon baking powder
1 egg, beaten
¾ cup milk
¼ cup vegetable oil
⅓ cup honey
1 teaspoon grated lemon peel

In a large bowl, combine the whole wheat flour, all-purpose flour, and baking powder. In a separate bowl, mix together the egg, milk, oil, honey, and lemon peel; add to the flour mixture. Stir until just moist. Fill greased muffin cups about ⅔ full with the batter. Bake in a preheated 400°F oven for 20-25 minutes. Cool on a wire rack for 5 minutes; remove from the pan. Makes 12 muffins.

Shredded Wheat Muffins

1½ cups shredded wheat cereal, finely rolled (about 1 cup crumbs)
1½ cups all-purpose flour
¼ cup sugar
2½ teaspoons baking powder
1 teaspoon cinnamon
½ cup raisins
2 eggs, beaten
¾ cup milk
¼ cup butter or margarine, melted
¼ cup honey
1 teaspoon grated lemon peel

🧁 In a large bowl, combine the cereal, flour, sugar, baking powder, cinnamon, and raisins. In a separate bowl, mix together the eggs, milk, butter, honey, and lemon peel; add to the flour mixture. Stir until just moist. Fill greased muffin cups about ⅔ full with the batter. Bake in a preheated 400°F oven for 20-25 minutes. Cool on a wire rack for 5 minutes; remove from the pan. Makes 12 muffins

Aloha Muffins

2 cups all-purpose flour
2 teaspoons baking powder
½ teaspoon baking soda
1 egg, beaten
¾ cup orange juice
¼ cup honey
1 tablespoon grated orange peel
¼ cup vegetable oil
½ cup shredded, unsweetened coconut
½ cup crushed, sweetened or unsweetened pineapple, well drained

In a large bowl, combine the flour, baking powder, and baking soda. In a separate bowl, mix together the egg, orange juice, honey, peel, oil, coconut, and pineapple; add to the flour mixture. Stir until just moist. Fill greased muffin cups about ⅔ full with the batter. Bake in a preheated 400°F oven for 20-25 minutes. Cool on a wire rack for 5 minutes; remove from the pan. Makes 12 muffins.

An excellent flavor combination.

Deluxe Chocolate Chip Muffins

2 cups all-purpose flour
1 teaspoon baking powder
1 teaspoon baking soda
½ cup butter or margarine
½ cup sugar
2 eggs
1 teaspoon vanilla extract
1 cup sour cream
1 cup chocolate chips
*Topping

In a large bowl, combine the flour, baking powder, and baking soda. In a separate bowl, cream together the butter and sugar; beat in the eggs and vanilla. Stir in the sour cream; mix well. Add to the flour mixture; stir until just moist. Fold in the chips. Fill greased muffin cups about ⅔ full with the batter. Sprinkle the Topping over the batter in each cup. Bake in a preheated 375°F oven for 20-25 minutes. Cool on a wire rack for 5 minutes; remove from the pan. Makes 12 muffins.

*<u>Topping</u>: In a small bowl, combine ½ cup chocolate chips, 1 tablespoon cocoa, ¼ cup all-purpose flour, and ¼ cup brown sugar. Cut in ¼ cup butter or margarine until crumbly.

Coffeecake Muffins

½ cup brown sugar
½ cup chopped walnuts
2 tablespoons all-purpose flour
1 teaspoon cinnamon
2 tablespoons butter or margarine, melted
1½ cups all-purpose flour
⅓ cup white sugar
2 teaspoons baking powder
¼ cup butter or margarine
1 egg, beaten
⅔ cup milk
1 teaspoon vanilla extract

① In a small bowl, stir together the brown sugar, nuts, 2 tablespoons flour, cinnamon, and 2 tablespoons melted butter; set aside. In a large bowl, combine the 1½ cups flour, white sugar, and baking powder. Using a pastry blender or fork, cut the ¼ cup of butter into the flour mixture until crumbly. Add the egg, milk, and vanilla; stir until just moist. Fill greased muffin cups about ⅓ full with the batter. Add about 2 teaspoons of the nut mixture to each cup; top with the remaining batter to fill each cup ⅔ full. Sprinkle the remaining nut mixture over the batter in each cup.

Bake in a preheated 375°F oven for 20 minutes. Cool on a wire rack for 5 minutes; remove from the pan. Makes 12 muffins.

Serve warm from the oven at your next Sunday brunch. Good served plain or with a pat of butter.

Fruit Cocktail Muffins

2 cups all-purpose flour
$\frac{1}{4}$ cup sugar
1 tablespoon baking powder
$\frac{1}{2}$ teaspoon nutmeg
1 teaspoon grated lemon peel
1 can (8 ounces) fruit cocktail
1 egg
$\frac{1}{3}$ cup vegetable oil
$\frac{1}{2}$ cup chopped walnuts
3 tablespoons sugar
1 teaspoon cinnamon

In a large bowl, combine the flour, $\frac{1}{4}$ cup sugar, baking powder, nutmeg, and lemon peel. Drain the fruit cocktail, reserving the syrup. Add enough water to the syrup to make $\frac{3}{4}$ cup. In a separate bowl, beat together the reserved syrup, egg, and oil. Add to the flour mixture; stir until just moist. Fold in the fruit and nuts. Fill greased muffin cups about $\frac{2}{3}$ full with the batter. Combine the remaining 3 tablespoons sugar and cinnamon; sprinkle over the batter in each cup. Bake in a preheated 400°F oven for 20-25 minutes. Cool on a wire rack for 5 minutes; remove from the pan. Makes 12 muffins.

Delicious served warm with whipped cream cheese.

Stuffed Gingerbread Muffins

1 cup boiling water
½ cup unsulphured molasses
2 cups all-purpose flour
1 teaspoon baking soda
1 teaspoon ginger
½ teaspoon cinnamon
¼ teaspoon nutmeg
½ cup chopped walnuts or pecans
½ cup butter or margarine
¼ cup brown sugar
2 eggs
6 large marshmallows, cut in half

Pour the boiling water over the molasses;

cool. In a large bowl, combine the flour, baking soda, ginger, cinnamon, nutmeg, and nuts. In a separate bowl, cream together the butter and brown sugar; beat in the eggs; stir in the molasses mixture. Add to the flour mixture; stir until just moist. Fill greased muffin cups $\frac{2}{3}$ full with the batter. Gently press a marshmallow half into the batter in each cup. Bake in a preheated 400°F oven for 20-25 minutes. Cool on a wire rack for 5 minutes; remove from the pan. Makes 12 muffins.

A surprise stuffing makes these moist muffins a special treat.

Glazed Lemon Nut Muffins

2 cups all-purpose flour
1/3 cup sugar
2 teaspoons baking powder
1 tablespoon grated lemon peel
1/2 cup chopped nuts
1 egg
1 cup milk
1/3 cup butter or margarine, melted
*Glaze

In a large bowl, combine the flour, sugar, baking powder, lemon peel, and nuts. In a separate bowl, beat together the egg, milk, and butter; add to the flour mixture. Stir until just moist. Fill greased muffin cups about 2/3 full with the batter. Bake in a preheated 400°F oven for 20-25 minutes. Carefully spoon the Glaze over the hot muffins. Cool on a wire rack for 10 minutes; remove from the pan. Makes 12 muffins.

*<u>Glaze</u>: In a small bowl, mix together 3 tablespoons lemon juice and 3 tablespoons confectioners' sugar until smooth.

Mincemeat Muffins

1½ cups all-purpose flour
½ cup rolled oats
¼ cup brown sugar
2 teaspoons baking powder
½ teaspoon baking soda
2 eggs
¾ cup milk
⅓ cup butter or margarine, melted
¾ cup prepared mincemeat
½ cup chopped nuts

In a large bowl, combine the flour, oats, sugar, baking powder, and baking soda. In a separate bowl, beat together the eggs, milk, and butter; add to the flour mixture. Stir until just moist. Stir in the mincemeat and nuts. Fill greased muffin cups about ⅔ full with the batter. Bake in a preheated 375°F oven for 20-25 minutes. Cool on a wire rack for 5 minutes; remove from the pan. Makes 12 muffins.

Frost with whipped cream cheese.

Peanut Butter Muffins

½ cup yellow cornmeal
1½ cups all-purpose flour
¼ cup brown sugar
1 tablespoon baking powder
½ cup peanut butter
1 cup milk
1 egg
3 tablespoons vegetable oil
½ cup chopped peanuts (optional)

In a large bowl, combine the cornmeal, flour, brown sugar, and baking powder. In a separate bowl, mix the peanut butter and ½ cup of the milk until smooth. Beat in the egg, oil, and remaining ½ cup milk. Add to the flour mixture; stir until just moist. Fill greased muffin cups about ⅔ full with the batter. Sprinkle the peanuts over the batter in each cup. Bake in a preheated 400°F oven for 20-25 minutes. Cool on a wire rack for 5 minutes; remove from the pan. Makes 12 muffins.

You can use chocolate chips instead of peanuts

Basic Muffin and Variations

2 cups all-purpose flour
$\frac{1}{4}$ cup sugar
2 teaspoons baking powder
$\frac{1}{2}$ teaspoon salt (optional)
1 egg
1 cup milk
$\frac{1}{4}$ cup butter or margarine, melted

In a large bowl, combine the flour, sugar, baking powder, and salt. In a separate bowl, beat together the egg, milk, and butter. Add to the flour mixture; stir until just moist. Fill greased muffin cups about $\frac{2}{3}$ full with the batter. Bake in a preheated 400°F oven for 20-25 minutes. Cool on a wire rack for 5 minutes; remove from the pan. Makes 12 muffins.

<u>Variations</u>: Gently fold any of the following ingredients into the basic batter: $\frac{1}{2}$ cup chopped dried fruit (dates, figs, apricots, apple rings, etc.); 1-2 teaspoons dried herbs; $\frac{1}{2}$ cup roasted sunflower seeds; 1 cup fresh seedless green grapes, cut in half; $\frac{1}{2}$ cup shredded cheese.

Savory Cheddar Muffins

2 cups all-purpose flour
1 tablespoon baking powder
1 teaspoon paprika
¼ cup butter or margarine
1 egg, beaten
1 cup milk
1 cup grated, sharp cheddar cheese

In a large bowl, combine the flour, baking powder, and paprika. Using a pastry blender or fork, cut the butter into the flour mixture until crumbly. Add the egg and milk; stir until just moist. Stir in the cheese. Fill greased muffin cups ⅔ full with the batter. Bake in a preheated 400°F oven for 20-25 minutes. Cool on a wire rack for 5 minutes; remove from the pan. Makes 12 muffins.

Serve these easy-to-make muffins with a bowl of spicy chili and a tossed green salad.